DATE DUE			

612.3
RIS

164843

Rissman, Rebecca.

My food pyramid

Healthy Eating

My Food Pyramid

Rebecca Rissman

Heinemann Library
Chicago, Illinois

www.heinemannraintree.com
Visit our website to find out
more information about
Heinemann-Raintree books.

To order:

☎ Phone 888-454-2279
💻 Visit www.heinemannraintree.com
to browse our catalog and order online.

Edited by Rebecca Rissman and Catherine Veitch
Designed by Joanna Hinton-Malivoire
Picture research by Elizabeth Alexander
Production by Victoria Fitzgerald
Originated by Capstone Global Library Ltd
Printed and bound in China by South China Printing Company Ltd

15 14 13 12 11 10
10 9 8 7 6 5 4 3 2 1

Library of Congress Cataloging-in-Publication Data
Rissman, Rebecca.
  My food pyramid / Rebecca Rissman.
    p. cm. -- (Healthy eating)
  Includes bibliographical references and index.
  ISBN 978-1-4329-3983-0 (hc) -- ISBN 978-1-4329-3990-8 (pb) 1.
Nutrition--Juvenile literature. 2. Food--Juvenile literature. I. Title.
  QP141.D488 2011
  612.3--dc22
                        2009052659

Acknowledgments
We would like to thank the following for permission to reproduce
photographs: © Capstone Publishers pp. **5, 6, 8, 10, 11, 12, 13, 14,
15, 17, 18,
19, 23 bottom** (Karon Dubke); Getty Images p. **7** (MIXA); Shutterstock
pp. **9**
(© Kzenon), **21** (© Jane September), **23 top** (© Jane September), **23
middle**
(© Kzenon); USDA Center for Nutrition Policy and Promotion pp. **4, 16,
20, 22.**

Back cover photograph of a boy looking at a food pyramid reproduced
with permission of © Capstone Publishers (Karon Dubke).

We would like to thank Nancy Harris and Dr. Matt Siegel for their
invaluable help in the preparation of this book.

Every effort has been made to contact copyright holders of material
reproduced in this book. Any omissions will be rectified in subsequent
printings if notice is given to the publishers.

Contents

My Food Pyramid

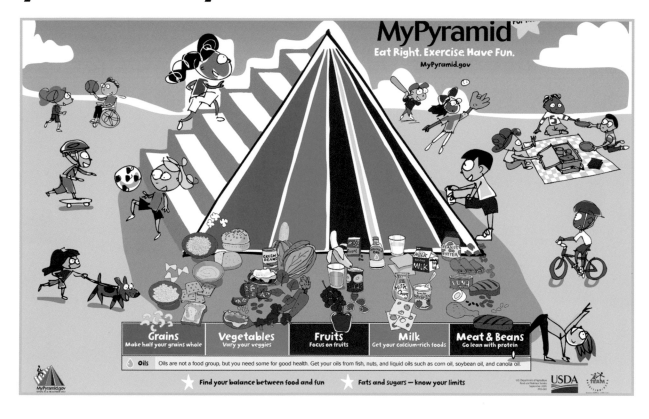

The food pyramid shows us how to stay healthy.

The food pyramid shows us what to eat to stay healthy.

Food Groups

There are five food groups.

We need to eat foods from each food group.

Foods from each food group give us nutrients.

Nutrients are parts of food that help us stay healthy.

Grains are a food group.

Bread, pasta, and rice are in this

food group.

Fruits are a food group. Apples, bananas, and oranges are in this food group.

Vegetables are a food group.
Broccoli, peppers, and carrots are in
this food group.

Milk is a food group. Milk, cheese, and yogurt are in this food group.

Meat and beans are a food group.
Chicken, beef, pork, fish, and beans
are in this food group.

Foods like sugar and oils are not food groups. You should eat few foods with sugar and oil each day.

Using the Food Pyramid

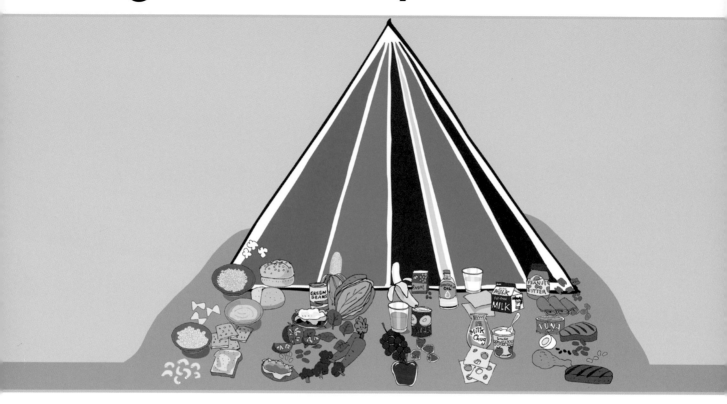

The food pyramid shows us how much to eat from each food group every day.

We should eat lots of vegetables,
fruits, grains, and milk.

We should eat some healthy meat and beans.

We should eat few oils and sugars.

Exercise

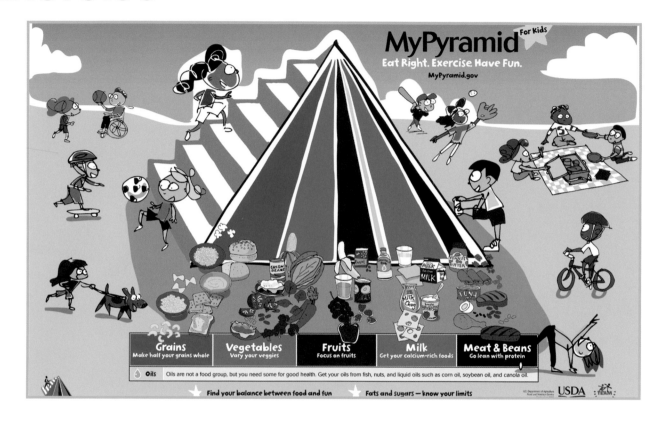

The food pyramid also shows people exercising.

This is to remind us to exercise.

We should be active every day.

Quiz

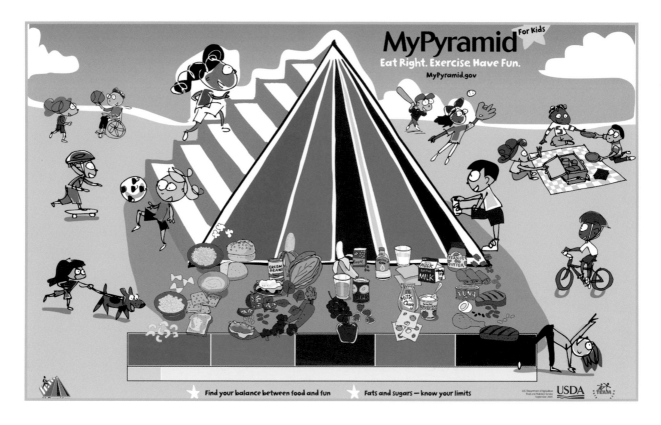

Can you name the food groups on the food pyramid?

Answer on page 24.

Picture Glossary

exercise busy doing a lot of things

healthy fit and well

nutrient parts in food that help to keep you healthy

Index

Answer to quiz on page 22: The food groups from left to right are grains, vegetables, fruits, milk, meat and beans.

Notes to Parents and Teachers

Before Reading

Tell children that eating healthy foods helps people to stay well. Explain that there are different food groups that contain different types of healthy foods. Write the five food groups on the board: meat and beans, fruits, vegetables, milk, and grains.

After Reading

• Place children into five groups, and assign each group one food group. Ask each group to make a list of different foods in that group. Then have each group report back to the class all the foods they listed.

• Explain to children that oils and sugars are types of foods that should be eaten sparingly. Show children photos of different foods and ask them to spot the foods with the most sugars and oils.